out of
the fifties –
into the sixties

6 FIGURATIVE EXPRESSIONISTS

march 15 – may 5, 2001

MICHAEL ROSENFELD GALLERY
NEW YORK

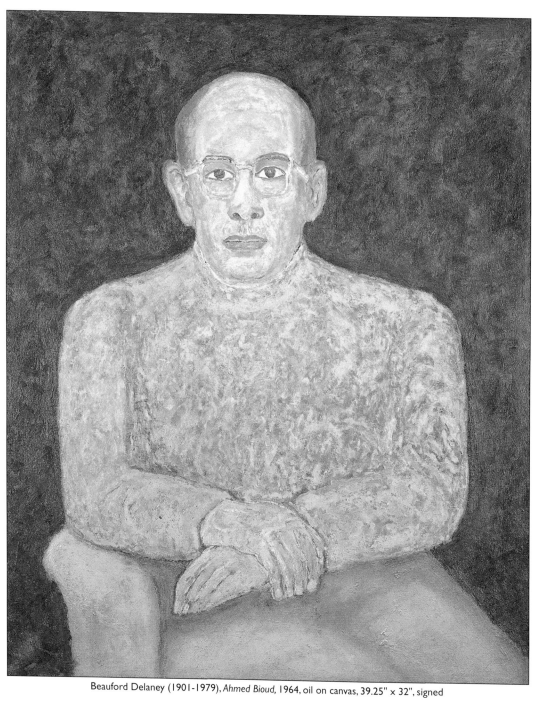

Beauford Delaney (1901-1979), *Ahmed Bioud,* 1964, oil on canvas, 39.25" x 32", signed

OUT OF THE FIFTIES — INTO THE SIXTIES

Out of the Fifties — Into the Sixties: 6 Figurative Expressionists explores six painters — Beauford Delaney, Leon Golub, Red Grooms, Lester Johnson, Jan Müller and Bob Thompson — who rejected the tenets of abstract expressionism and embraced the human figure to create powerful and disparate visual statements. While not encyclopedic, this exhibition presents a microcosm of a much-overlooked aesthetic in American art that falls chronologically between Abstract Expressionism and Pop Art.

In the 1950s, a trend toward figurative expressionism emerged in American art as a reaction to the dominance of abstract expressionism that began to establish itself during the late-1940s. Many artists and critics, most notably Clement Greenberg, dogmatically believed in the omnipotence of abstract expressionism. To them, abstract expressionism was the only viable universal language that permitted artists to address profound existential concerns in the post-World-War-II era. In addition, they believed that abstract expressionism transcended representational imagery; images of man were outmoded and, ultimately, an inadequate means of artistic expression.

However, for the six artists in this exhibition, the human form was an evocative subject and the basis of their imagery. These figurative expressionists, like others, believed abstraction and figuration need not be mutually exclusive, and they combined the two, creating provocative figurative paintings with expressive, gestural brushstrokes. In 1954, Jan Müller expressed a sentiment shared by the artists in this exhibition, "Abstraction is no longer enough for me. So, I'm returning to the image — the image gives one a wider sense of communication."

Figurative expressionist painters of the 1950s had few exhibition opportunities until they banded together and opened alternative spaces. In 1952, artists Wolf Kahn and Felix Pasilis opened the artist's cooperative Hansa Gallery in a downtown loft on 12th Street. In its eight years, Hansa Gallery hosted numerous performances and lectures. The gallery also mounted over seventy–five individual exhibitions including a 1958 memorial exhibition for Jan Müller. Inspired by the success of Hansa Gallery and in rebellion against the 'establishment' located on Tenth Street, Red Grooms and Jay Milder opened City Gallery in 1958, in Grooms' downtown loft. One year after its establishment, Grooms opened the Delancey Street Museum, exhibiting — among others — Bob Thompson, Lester Johnson, Claes Oldenburg and Jim Dine. Outside of the New York downtown scene, the Sun Gallery in Provincetown, Massachusetts became a significant venue for the figurative expressionists. Opened in the summer of 1955 by Dominic Val Falcone and Yvonne Anderson, the Sun Gallery staged some of the earliest "happenings" and exhibited Red Grooms, Bob Thompson and Lester Johnson.

In the late-1950s, figurative expressionism experienced a rise to prominence with a flurry of museum exhibitions. Landmark exhibitions included: *The New York School: Second Generation Paintings by Twenty-three Artists* (The Jewish Museum, 1957), *New Images of Man* (The Museum of Modern Art, 1959), *Figure in Contemporary*

American Painting (The American Federation of Arts, 1960), The Emerging Figure (The Museum of Contemporary Art, Houston, 1961), Jan Müller: Retrospective (The Solomon R. Guggenheim Museum, 1962), Recent Painting U.S.A: The Figure (The Museum of Modern Art, 1962) and The Figure International (The American Federation of Arts, 1965).

A resurgence of interest in figurative expressionism from the 1950s and 1960s was spurred in more recent years by the exhibition The Figurative Fifties: New York Expressionism organized by The Newport Harbor Art Museum. This 1988 exhibition focused on painters active in New York, but the movement of figurative expressionism was not limited to the east coast. By including Leon Golub and expatriate Beauford Delaney, Out of the Fifties — Into the Sixties suggests the geographic range of artists who embraced figurative expressionism. Although Red Grooms, Lester Johnson, Jan Müller and Bob Thompson predominantly worked in New York, Golub and Delaney spent a significant part of their careers outside of the city. Golub began his career in Chicago but lived in the late-1950s and early 1960s in Paris before settling in New York in 1964. In 1953, Beauford Delaney moved from New York to Paris, where he remained until his death in 1979. Of course, figurative expressionism flourished elsewhere, particularly in San Francisco, which was home to numerous figurative painters, including Richard Diebenkorn and David Park.

For the past few decades, there has been a tendency to narrowly define the 1950s through Abstract Expressionism and the 1960s through Pop Art. It is my hope that Out of the Fifties — Into the Sixties: 6 Figurative Expressionists will broaden the story of art by helping to make a place for the figurative expressionists.

Michael Rosenfeld, March 2001

Bob Thompson (1937-1966), Self-Portrait, 1964-65, oil on canvas, 16" x 13.25", signed

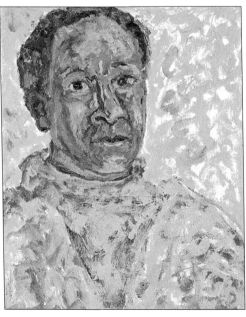

Beauford Delaney (1901-1979), Self-Portrait, 1964, oil on canvas, 16" x 13", signed

Lester Johnson (b.1919), *Untitled*, 1963, oil on canvas, 66" x 44", signed

BEAUFORD DELANEY
(1901-1979)

Beauford Delaney, born in Knoxville, Tennessee, studied with a local artist before moving to Boston in 1923 to study at the Massachusetts Normal Art School, the Copley Society and the South Boston School of Art. In Boston, Delaney was exposed to black activist politics through his association with some of the most radical African-Americans of the time including Countee Cullen and William Monroe Trotter. In 1929, Delaney moved to New York City and began painting strong portraits of members of the New York elite and notables such as Marion Anderson, Ethel Waters and Duke Ellington. In 1930, Delaney studied at the Art Students League with John Sloan and Thomas Hart Benton and met among others Richmond Barthé, Charles Alston and James A. Porter. Interested in all the arts including poetry and jazz, Delaney formed life-long friendships with James Baldwin, Palmer Hayden, Al Hirshfeld, Henry Miller, Alfred Steiglitz and Ellis Wilson. Delaney's paintings of the 1940s and early 1950s consist largely of modernist interiors and street scenes, executed in impasto with broad areas of vibrant colors. In 1953, Delaney left New York and his Greene Street studio and traveled to Europe, settling in Paris. Feeling free of racial and sexual biases, Delaney expanded his painting vocabulary and began to create lyrical, colorful non-objective abstractions. These paintings, consisting of elaborate, fluid swirls of paint applied in luminous hues, are pure and simplified expressions of light; the essence of Delaney's art. For Delaney abstraction was "the penetration of something that is more profound in many ways than the rigidity of a form." In 1978, The Studio Museum in Harlem organized his first major retrospective exhibition which included abstractions and portraits completed in Paris. A 1968 recipient of a National Council of the Arts Grant, Delaney's work is included in numerous museum collections. In 1979, Delaney died in Paris while hospitalized for mental illness.

Beauford Delaney (1901-1979), *Bernard Hassell,* c.1962, oil on canvasboard, 25.5" x 21.25"

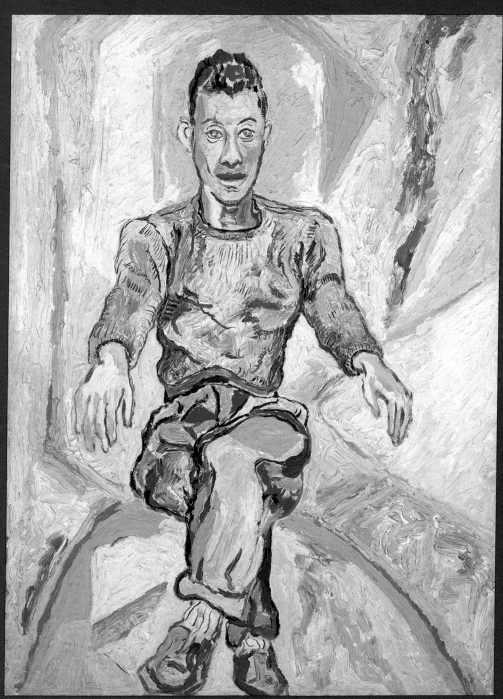

Beauford Delaney (1901-1979), *James Baldwin*, c.1955, oil on canvasboard, 24" x 18"

c. 1962-63. Courtesy of the Artist

"as to the particular nature of my art: in making what i find necessary to make, i seem to (and thereby wish to) portray a cryptic, vehement, and often tragic image of man. this is not necessarily the "everyday" image but introspections into some aspects of a more ultimate realization of role. i admire greek tragedy and, such writers as kafka and joyce. i seek images perhaps powerful and awesome, at times eroded and isolated, perhaps anomalous — an ambiguity of tradition and the irrational that yet resonates of common experience."

Artist Statement, 1956. Quoted in the exhibition catalogue
Leon Golub, Malmö Konsthall, 1993, p.69.

leon golub

(b.1922)

"All art is political," states Leon Golub, who for the last five decades has examined male power and aggression in his heroic paintings. Born in Chicago, Illinois, Golub, a member of "Monster Roster," a group of Chicago artists who rejected the rise of abstract expressionism and embraced unconventional life forms, studied at the University of Chicago (1940-42) and the School of the Art Institute of Chicago (1946-50). In 1956 and again in 1959, Golub traveled to Europe with his wife, artist Nancy Spero, spending five years in Paris (1959-1964). In 1964, Golub and Spero returned to the United States and settled in New York City, where they remain today. Rooted in classicism and inspired by tribal art, art of the insane, photography and broadcast media, Golub has consistently confronted violence — battles, combat, invasions, torture, interrogation and assassination — in his paintings, drawings and printmaking but by blurring the distinction between the protagonist and the antagonist, Golub has attempted to remain impartial. Beginning in 1950, Golub developed a labor-intensive painting process to build surface texture; he applies successive layers of lacquer or acrylic and then removes or carves into them with solvents or scraping tools like meat cleavers. Interested in a 'sculptural' image of man, Golub began in 1964-65 to mutilate his mural sized canvases, cutting them into irregular forms after painting was completed. Between 1976-1979, he focused almost exclusively on portraiture, capturing approximately 100 men of power including Henry Kissinger, Ho Chi Minh and Fidel Castro. In the 1980s, he returned to social commentary, investigating racial and urban tensions and beginning in the mid-1990s, his provocative imagery has been wedded to language inspired from graffiti. Throughout the years, Golub has been an active public speaker, critic, theorist and educator, teaching at Rutgers University (1971-1991). A recipient of numerous awards of distinction, Golub has had over sixty individual museum exhibitions. Currently his work is the subject of a traveling retrospective organized by the Irish Museum of Modern Art in Dublin.

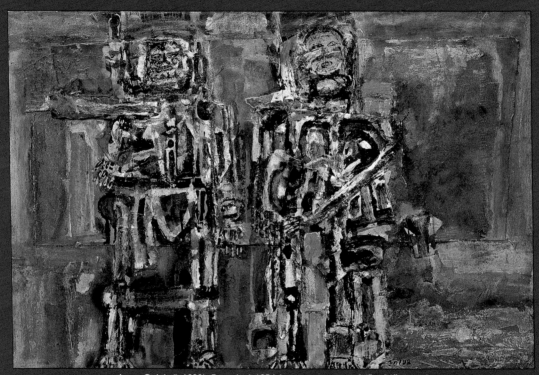

Leon Golub (b.1922), *Entombed*, 1954, lacquer on canvas, 24" x 36", signed

Leon Golub (b.1922), *Head I*, 1966, acrylic on linen, 32.25" x 36", signed

14

Excerpted from *Red Grooms: A Retrospective*, The Pennsylvania Academy
of the Fine Arts, 1985, p.17.

RED GROOMS

(b.1937)

Recognized today as a pioneer of site-specific sculpture and installation art, Red
Grooms (born Charles Rogers Grooms in Nashville, Tennessee) had an early interest
in drawing, attending classes locally at the Children's Museum and privately with artists
Juanita Green Williams and Joseph Van Sickle. A self-proclaimed "restless and undisci-
plined student," Grooms studied briefly at the Art Institute of Chicago (1955), The New
School of Social Research in New York City (1956) and at Hans Hofmann's legendary
summer school in Provincetown, Massachusetts (1956). In 1957, Grooms moved to
New York City but returned to Provincetown in summers, where he exhibited at The
Sun Gallery, an innovative space that consistently featured young figurative expressionists including Mary Frank, Alex Katz, Lucas Samaras, Jan Müller and Bob Thompson.
It was here that he also staged his first of many Happenings, *Play Called Fire*. Labeled a
beatnik artist, who was part of a "junk art" movement, Grooms opened the first alternative exhibition space, City Gallery, in 1958 with artist Jay Milder. City Gallery was
located in Groom's downtown loft, and a year after its establishment, Grooms opened
the Delancey Street Museum. In 1960, Grooms moved to Italy for eighteen months,
where he made his first film, *The Unwelcome Guests*, with his wife Mimi Gross. Returning
to New York in 1962, he continued in his paintings, drawings, "stick-outs" and collages
to document the figure in urban America with humor and irony, rejecting the sterile and
detached look of the Pop art phenomenon. In 1975-76, Grooms and a construction
crew completed and exhibited *Ruckus Manhattan*, twelve detailed sculptural environ-
ments capturing specific landmarks in Manhattan. Over the last four decades, Grooms
has created a large body of work and has had numerous individual exhibitions including a traveling retrospective organized by The Pennsylvania Academy of the Fine Arts in
1985, and his work has inspired audiences at home and abroad. He lives and continues
to work in New York City.

Red Grooms (b.1937), *Three Bathers*, 1959, oil and cardboard on canvas, 35" x 66.25", signed

Red Grooms (b.1937), *Gaugin*, 1963, oil on canvas, 30" x 30", signed

18

"There is no balance in my paintings because balance seems to me to be static. Life, which I try to reflect in my paintings, is dynamic...To me, my paintings are action paintings – paintings that move across the canvas, paintings that do not get stuck, but flow like time."

Excerpted from *Lester Johnson: The Kaleidoscopic Crowd, Paintings 1970-1974*, David Anderson Publications, 1975, p.14-15.

LESTER JOHNSON

(b.1919)

Lester Johnson, born in Minneapolis, Minnesota, studied at the Minneapolis School of Art with Alexander Masley, at the St. Paul School of Art with Cameron Booth and later at the Art Institute of Chicago (1942-47). In 1947, he moved to New York City, attended classes at the Hofmann School of Fine Arts and shared a lower east side loft with Larry Rivers. Three years later, he shared studio space with Philip Pearlstein. A member of the Eighth Street Club, Johnson had his first solo exhibition in 1951 at the Artist's Gallery. His work of the late-1940s was predominantly pure form or "action painting" with an undertone of content that soon evolved in the mid-1950s into figurative painting. Early figures were dark, anonymous silhouettes, painted thickly with expressive gestural strokes and drips. Over the years, as the process of painting became more of a physical act for Johnson, his style became increasingly free and his emphasis shifted from physical form to the psychological content of his subjects. Johnson was greatly inspired by the movement of the city streets, and particularly the "bums" he watched near his Bowery Street studio. From 1958 to 1959, Johnson taught painting classes and along with Claes Oldenburg, Jim Dine and Bob Thompson, exhibited at City Gallery, an alternative exhibition space opened by Red Grooms and Jay Milder. Throughout the last four decades, Johnson has continued to explore the human condition and in his paintings and drawings, he has attempted to "prove that man is more than a man." In 1964, he was appointed Professor of Art at Yale University and from 1969-74, served as Director of Studies for Yale's School of Art and Architecture. In 1966, after relocating to Milford, Connecticut, Johnson experienced a tragic fire in his studio and over six hundred works were destroyed. A recipient of numerous honors of distinction including a Guggenheim Fellowship in Painting (1973), Johnson was elected to the National Academy of Design in 1987. He lives and continues to work in Connecticut.

Lester Johnson (b.1919), *Untitled (Head)*, 1962, oil on canvasboard, 18" x 14", signed

Lester Johnson (b.1919), *Untitled (Portrait Ochre)*, 1963, oil on canvas, 70" x 48", signed

"IN OUR AGE THE ARTIST CANNOT TAKE FLIGHT FROM THE ROTTENNESS OF SOCIETY TO PORTRAY JUST THE SPIRIT OF MAN. HE HAS A RESPONSIBILITY TOWARD THAT STENCH IF ANY AWARENESS AND MUST TRY TO REACH THE MORE SOCIAL POSITION IN HIS ETHICAL AND MORAL EVALUATION OF LIFE. HE SHOULD PORTRAY LIFE, BUT AS LIFE OF POSSIBILITY NOT THE REFUGE AND WELL-BEING STIMULATED BY ACROBATICS WITHOUT CONTENT. HE HAS TO FIND A WAY TO THE CLOSER RELATIONSHIP AMONG THINGS AND HAS TO BECOME AWARE OF MAN'S MULTIPLE SENSITIVENESS NOT JUST TIED DOWN TO THE STRING OF AN APRON OF ONE THING CALLED PURITY IN OUR AGE. BUT WHAT IS PURITY, PERFECTION OR A MULTITUDE OF IDEAS?"

Quoted from the artist's 1956 notebook. Excerpted from
New Images of Man, The Museum of Modern Art, 1959, p.106.

JAN MÜLLER
(1922-1958)

Born in Hamburg, Germany, Jan Müller immigrated to the United States in 1941 after having survived Nazi Germany by living for periods in Prague, rural Switzerland, Amsterdam, Paris and Portugal. For years while living in New York City, Müller worked odd jobs before discovering painting in 1945. Müller first studied for six months at The Art Students League in New York and later with Hans Hofmann from 1945-1950 at his School of Fine Arts. Greatly influenced by Hofmann and German expressionism, Müller developed a style of abstract painting, embracing almost exclusively the form of the square (oddly or perfectly shaped) in orderly compositions. However, in 1954, Müller abandoned geometric order and adopted a more figurative language, integrating the figure with literature and mythology. In his heroic thematic compositions often populated with witches, angels, demons and naked figures, Müller explored Faust legends, religious narratives of the German Middle Ages and great literature including Shakespeare, Goethe and The Bible. Labeled an "authentic expressionist" who painted with fury in heavy impastos, Müller was a founding member of the Hansa Gallery in 1952, along with Jean Follett, Wolf Kahn, Allan Kaprow and Richard Stankiewicz. His first solo exhibition was in 1953 at Hansa Gallery, where he exhibited consecutively from 1953 to 1958 at its space on East 12th Street. Müller spent the summers of 1950, 1951 and 1952 in Provincetown, Massachusetts, returning once more in the summer of 1955 when he began his series of "path" paintings. Müller became a United States citizen in 1957. At the age of thirty-nine, Müller died; his heart had been weakened by his chronic battle with rheumatic fever from the age of thirteen. In 1959, his work was included in the landmark exhibition *New Images of Man* at the Museum of Modern Art and in 1962, The Solomon R. Guggenheim Museum in cooperation with the Institute of Contemporary Art in Boston presented a retrospective exhibition, the first museum solo exhibition of his work. In subsequent years, Müller's work has been included in numerous museum exhibitions including *The Figurative Fifties* organized by The Newport Harbor Art Museum.

Jan Müller (1922-1958), *The Trysting Place*, c.1957, oil on canvas, 45" x 42"

Jan Müller (1922-1958), *The Search for the Unicorn*, 1957, oil on canvas, 70" x 93"

"I CANNOT FIND A PLACE NOR CATEGORY IN WHICH TO PUT MY PAINTINGS NOR A NAME TO CALL THEM....MY SOMETHINGS HAVE BEEN AND ARE OFTEN THOUGHT OF AS SPREADING OF EMOTIONAL JAMS....MY AIM IS TO PROJECT IMAGES THAT SEEM VITAL TO ME, NEVER TO MAKE PAINTINGS THAT CONFORM TO THE VISION OF EVERYONE. MY PROBLEM IS THE PROJECTION OF IMAGES [OFTEN ELUSIVE] THAT SEEM TO HAVE MEANING IN TERMS OF FEELING-DEPTH RESPONSE. THE IMPORTANT THING IS TO TRANSFER THE IMAGE TO THE CANVAS AS IT APPEARS TO ME; TO MODIFY THE WOULD-BE FALLACIOUS. THEREFORE, I MUST ACCEPT IT ON APPEARANCE. MY PAINTING HAS NO STYLE—IT CONSTANTLY CHANGES—SIMPLY DIFFERENT IMAGES. MY CRITERION IS THE INTEGRITY OF THE PROJECTION. I LOVE ALL THINGS THAT LOOK THE WAY I FEEL!"

Quoted in "Academic Straight Jacket: Disdainful Thompson,"
Gazette of the Arts in Louisville, February 9, 1959, p.l.

bob THOMPSON

(1937-1966)

Bob Thompson, born in Louisville, Kentucky studied at Boston University (1955-56) and the University of Louisville (1957-58) with German expressionist Ulfert Wilke. After completing his sophomore year, Thompson spent the summer of 1958 in Provincetown, where he was introduced to the expressive figurative work of Jan Müller, Hans Hofmann and Red Grooms. In the fall of 1958, Thompson moved to New York and embraced a Bohemian life-style, forming friendships with jazz musicians, writers, poets and fellow artists including Ornette Coleman, Charlie Haden, Leroi Jones, Ted Jones and Jay Milder. A regular at the infamous jazz club the Five Spot, Thompson participated in two of the earliest Happenings staged in the United States: Allan Kaprow's *18 Happenings in 6 Parts* and Red Grooms' *The Burning Building.* In 1960, he had his first solo exhibition in New York at the Delancey Street Museum and in 1963, artist Lester Johnson introduced him to Martha Jackson of the Martha Jackson Gallery, New York, where he had solo exhibitions in 1963 and 1965. Thompson traveled extensively and spent time in London (1960), Paris (1961-62), Ibiza (1962-63) and Rome (1965-66), where he died tragically short of his twenty-ninth birthday. Known for a language of expressive landscapes and figures painted in hot, violent tones, Thompson's paintings wed his own visionary style with compositional schemes derived from classical predecessors like Titian, Goya and Bosch. Declared by Allen Ginsberg as "the most original visionary painter of his days, a first *natural* American psychedelic colorist," Thompson succeeded in producing a distinctive body of work which stands very much alone in 20th century art. In 1978, The Studio Museum in Harlem organized his first retrospective exhibition and in 1998, The Whitney Museum of American Art organized and traveled his second.

Bob Thompson (1937-1966), *Black Monster,* 1959, oil on canvas, 56" x 67", signed

Bob Thompson (1937-1966), *La Mort des Enfant de Bethel*, 1964-65, oil on canvas, 23" x 35", signed

CREDITS

Exhibition Coordinator
Michael Rosenfeld

**Catalogue Design
and Editor**
halley k harrisburg

Editorial Assistant
Jessica Scarlata

Research Assistant
Karlyn Benson

Catalogue Photography
Josh Nefsky
p.12 David Reynolds

**Catalogue Art Direction
and Production**
CP Design

Catalogue Typefaces
Gill Sans, Pushpin, Moondog,
Scripto, Recordhop, BigBeat,
Dinette

Catalogue Printing
Oceanic Graphic Printing, Inc.

**Printed in China
Edition 2000**

ISBN 1-930416-09-1

© Michael Rosenfeld Gallery
24 West 57 Street, 7th Floor
New York, NY 10019
(212) 247-0082
(212) 247-0402 fax

www.michaelrosenfeldart.com

Gallery Hours:
Tuesday through Saturday
10:00-6:00

Photographs, reproduction rights
and research assistance were gra-
ciously provided by Luis Accorsi,
Robert Buck, Tom Burkhardt,
Ronald Feldman Fine Arts, Leon
Golub, Red Grooms, Wolf Kahn,
Samm Kunce, Marlborough
Gallery, Fred W. McDarrah, Martica
Sawin, Carol Thompson, TimePix
and Judith Wilson.

EXHIBITION CHECKLIST

Beauford Delaney (1901-1979)
Ahmed Bioud, 1964
oil on canvas
39.25" x 32", signed

Beauford Delaney (1901-1979)
Bernard Hassell, c.1962
oil on canvas
25.5" x 21.25"

Beauford Delaney (1901-1979)
James Baldwin, c.1955
oil on canvasboard
24" x 18"

Beauford Delaney (1901-1979)
Self-Portrait, 1964
oil on canvas
16" x 13", signed
Tennessee State Museum, purchased in part
through funds from the Judith Rothschild
Foundation

Leon Golub (b.1922)
Entombed, 1954
lacquer on canvas
24" x 36", signed

Leon Golub (b.1922)
Head I, 1966
acrylic on linen
32.25" x 36", signed

Leon Golub (b.1922)
Le Combat VII, 1963
acrylic on canvas
51" x 80", signed

Red Grooms (b.1937)
Gaugin, 1963
oil on canvas
30" x 30", signed

Red Grooms (b.1937)
Three Bathers, 1959
oil and cardboard on canvas
35" x 66.25", signed

Lester Johnson (b.1919)
Untitled (Head), c.1961
oil on canvas
26" x 20", signed

Lester Johnson (b.1919)
Untitled (Head), 1962
oil on canvasboard
18" x 14", signed

Lester Johnson (b.1919)
Untitled, 1963
oil on canvas
66" x 44", signed

Lester Johnson (b.1919)
Untitled (Portrait Ochre), 1963
oil on canvas
70" x 48", signed

Jan Müller (1922-1958)
The Search for the Unicorn, 1957
oil on canvas
70" x 93", signed

Jan Müller (1922-1958)
The Trysting Place, c.1957
oil on canvas
45" x 42"

Bob Thompson (1937-1966)
Black Monster, 1959
oil on canvas
56" x 67", signed

Bob Thompson (1937-1966)
La Mort des Enfant de Bethel, 1964-65
oil on canvas
23" x 35", signed

Bob Thompson (1937-1966)
Self-Portrait, 1964-65
oil on canvas
16" x 13.25", signed

Bob Thompson (1937-1966)
Untitled, c.1960-64
oil on wood chair rails
Top: 2.5" x 12.5"
Middle: 3" x 12.5"
Bottom: 3.25" x 13"

MICHAEL ROSENFELD GALLERY PUBLICATIONS

Abstraction Across America, 1934-1946, AAA and Transcendentalists ....essays by Ed Garman and Hananiah Harari
African-American Art: 20th Century Masterworks ....essay by Beryl Wright
African-American Art: 20th Century Masterworks, II ....foreword by Harold B. Nelson, essay by Professor Richard J. Powell
African-American Art: 20th Century Masterworks, III ....essay by Michael Rosenfeld
African-American Art: 20th Century Masterworks, IV ....forewords by Kevin Grogan and Michael Rosenfeld
African-American Art: 20th Century Masterworks, V ....foreword by Nancy Corwin, essay by Dr. Leslie King-Hammond
African-American Art: 20th Century Masterworks, VI ....essay by Michael Rosenfeld
African-American Art: 20th Century Masterworks, VII ....foreword by Jeffrey Spalding, essay by halley k harrisburg
African-American Art: 20th Century Masterworks, VIII ....foreword by Dr. Alvia J. Wardlaw, statements by several artists
Aspects of American Abstraction: 1930-1942 ....essay by Dr. Gail Stavitsky
Benjamin Benno: 1930s American Modernist in Paris ....essay by Donna Gustafson
Byron Browne: Evolution of an American Modernist, 1930s-50s ....essay by Professor Matthew Baigell
Federico Castellon: Surrealist Paintings Rediscovered, 1933-1934 ....essay by Paul Cummings
Federico Castellon: Surrealist Drawings of the 1930s ....statement by Michael Rosenfeld
Counterpoints: American Art, 1930-1945 ....essay by Michael Rosenfeld
Defining the Edge: Early American Abstraction,
Selections from the Collection of Dr. Peter B. Fischer ....essay by Dr. Gail Stavitsky with selected artist quotes
Beauford Delaney: Liquid Light – Paris Abstractions, 1954-1970 ....essay by Professor David Leeming
Burgoyne Diller: Collages ....essay by Dr. Susan C. Larsen
Burgoyne Diller: The Third Dimension, Sculpture & Drawings, 1930-1965 ....essay by Michael Rosenfeld
Exploring the Unknown: Surrealism in American Art ....essay by Michael Rosenfeld
Essence of the Orb ....statement by Michael Rosenfeld with selected artist quotes
Fiber and Form: The Woman's Legacy ....foreword by halley k harrisburg
Morris Graves: Toward an Ultimate Reality ....selected artist quotes
Nancy Grossman: Loud Whispers, Four Decades of Assemblage, Collage and Sculpture ....foreword by Thomas Styron, essay by Dr. Lowery Stokes Sims
William H. Johnson: Works from the Collection of Mary Beattie Brady ....statement by Michael Rosenfeld with selected artist quotes
Blanche Lazzell: American Modernist ....essay by Michael Rosenfeld and halley k harrisburg
Norman Lewis ....selected artist quotes
Linear Impulse ....statement by Michael Rosenfeld with selected artist quotes
Lines & Myths: Abstraction in American Art, 1941-1951 ....essay by Professor Melvin P. Lader
Martha Madigan: Seeds of Light from the Human Nature Series ....essay by Charles Hagen
Boris Margo: Surrealism to Abstraction, 1932-1952 ....essay by Jeffrey Wechsler
Michael Rosenfeld Gallery: The First Decade ....essay by Michael Rosenfeld and halley k harrisburg
Clifford Odets: "In Hell + Why": Paintings on Paper ....essay by Michael Rosenfeld and Harold Clurman Odets' eulogy
Alfonso Ossorio: Reflection & Redemption - The Surrealist Decade ....essay by Professor Ellen Landau
Alfonso Ossorio: The Child Returns: 1950-Philippines, Expressionist Paintings on Paper ....essay by Dr. Francis V. O'Connor
Alfonso Ossorio: The Creeks: Before, During and After ....essay by Mike Solomon
Alfonso Ossorio: The Shingle Figures ....essay by B.H. Friedman
Out of the Fifties – Into the Sixties, 6 Figurative Expressionists ....essay by Michael Rosenfeld
Perceivable Realities: Eilshemius, Graves, Tanner, Tchelitchew ....statement by Michael Rosenfeld
Betye Saar: Workers + Warriors, The Return of Aunt Jemima ....essay by Dr. Arlene Raven
Betye Saar: A Version of Survival ....essay by Dr. Lizzetta LeFalle-Collins
Charles Seliger: Biomorphic Drawings, 1944-1947 ....essay by Sam Hunter
Charles Seliger: Infinities ....essay by Addison Parks
Charles Seliger: Nature's Journal ....essay by Professor Gail Levin
Charles Seliger: The Nascent Image – Recent Paintings ....foreword by Roald Hoffmann and an interview with the artist by halley k
                                                                                          harrisburg
Surrealism Embodied: The Figure in American Art, 1933-1953 ....essay by Jeffrey Wechsler
Lenore Tawney: Meditations – Assemblages, Collages & Weavings ....essay by Dr. Judith Stein
Pavel Tchelitchew: Nature Transformed ....interview with Charles Henri Ford by Paul Cummings
Pavel Tchelitchew: Nature Within & Without ....essay by Paul Cummings
Bob Thompson: Fantastic Visions, Paintings & Drawings ....statement by Carol Thompson
Bob Thompson: Heroes, Martyrs & Spectres ....statement by Michael Rosenfeld
The Transcendental Painting Group: Major Paintings ....essay by halley k harrisburg
True Grit ....essay by Dr. Arlene Raven
Charmion von Wiegand: Spirit & Form - Collages, 1946-1961 ....essay by Dr. Susan C. Larsen
Charmion von Wiegand: Spirituality in Abstraction, 1945-1969 ....essay by Dr. Jennifer Newton Hersh
The WPA Era: Urban Views & Visions ....essay by Dr. Francis V. O'Connor

MICHAEL ROSENFELD GALLERY EXHIBITION HISTORY